PASTA
MADE EASY

OTHER NO NONSENSE COOKING GUIDES

OTHER NO NONSENSE GUIDES

NO NONSENSE COOKING GUIDE®

PASTA MADE EASY

IRENA CHALMERS

WITH
MELANIE BARNARD AND BROOKE DOJNY

LONGMEADOW PRESS

PASTA MADE EASY

Copyright © 1989 by Irena Chalmers

Published by Longmeadow Press, 201 High Ridge Road, Stamford, Connecticut 06904. No part of this book may be reproduced or used in any form or by any means, electronic or mechanical, including photocopying, recording, or by an information storage and retrieval system, without permission in writing from the publisher.

No Nonsense Cooking Guide is a registered trademark of Longmeadow Press

ISBN 0-681-40700-X

Printed in the United States of America

0 9 8 7 6 5 4 3 2

STAFF FOR NO NONSENSE COOKING GUIDES

EDITORIAL DIRECTION: **Jean Atcheson**

MANAGING EDITOR: **Mary Goodbody**

COVER DESIGN: **Karen Skelton**

ART DIRECTION & DESIGN: **Helene Berinsky**

ASSISTANT EDITOR: **Maurice Goodbody**

COVER PHOTOGRAPH: **Matthew Klein**

TYPESETTING: **ComCom, Allentown, Pennsylvania**

CONTENTS

ACKNOWLEDGMENTS

Grateful acknowledgment is made to the following for permission to reproduce or adapt original recipes:

The Walnut Marketing Board; The Norway Sardine Industry

PASTA MADE EASY

We all share a love for pasta. Lifted from a pot of boiling water, quickly drained, tossed with sweet butter, a grinding of black pepper and a grating of cheese, just-cooked pasta is a glorious food. Good as it is when simply served with butter and cheese, it has the happiest way of lending itself to any number of recipes and treatments. We eat pasta hot and cold; blanketed with rich cream sauces, tomato sauces and chunky meat and seafood sauces; layered with cheeses and vegetables in casseroles; stirred into hearty, warming soups; and stuffed with heady, herb-scented fillings. However we choose to eat our pasta, it is always satisfying and delicious.

Pasta is made from flour, water and eggs (though a few pastas contain no eggs). Most is made with white flour, although semolina and durum flour are commonly used throughout Italy. Pastas made with whole wheat flour are sturdier than others. Some pastas are flavored with vegetables, such as spinach or carrots, which give them color and alter the taste a little. What brings about the biggest differences in pastas, however, is their shape.

The first pasta shapes that come to mind are strands. These include long, round spaghetti, thinner vermicelli, flat, narrow linguine and fettuccine, flat, wide lasagne and wispy, fine capellini and fidelini. The shaped pastas include shells, tubes, butterflies, wheels and twists as well as tiny grain-like orzo and pastina, used mainly in soup. Manicotti and cannelloni are large tubes designed for stuffing; sometimes they are made by rolling large flat squares or rectangles of dough around a filling.

Throughout the book we recommend certain pastas for each recipe, usually giving one or two alternatives. There is also an abbreviated glossary at the end of this introduction—abbreviated only because there are so many different pasta shapes that it would take many pages to cover them all.

Most people buy packaged dry pasta, and most of these products are very good indeed. These days, however, supermarkets and specialty stores are offering fresh pasta with greater frequency. This is pasta that has so recently been made that it has not had time to dry and harden. It cooks in a shorter period of time than packaged and many aficionados swear it tastes better, too. Dry, packaged pasta keeps for months and months in a well-ventilated cupboard; fresh pasta should be stored in the refrigerator and eaten within a day or two. It is possible to freeze fresh pasta for later use, or to let it dry completely and store it in a paper sack.

Anyone who prefers fresh to dry pasta will surely like homemade best of all. You cannot get fresher pasta and, as with making your own bread, there is a great deal of personal satisfaction to be had from "making it yourself." Hand-cranked pasta machines are inexpensive and easy to use. If you plan to make pasta frequently, it would be worth investing in one.

Freshly made pasta can be cooked immediately (some say this is the absolute best way to eat it), left for a few hours covered with a dish towel before cooking, or hung on wooden racks and allowed to dry completely. Dry pasta should be stored in a cool, dry cupboard packed loosely in a paper bag. Some cooks tie fresh pasta strands into a loose, figure-eight shaped knot and let it dry. This makes it easy to store and the knots can be tossed into boiling water, where they unravel very nicely as they cook.

Most pasta cooks recommend that pasta be cooked in six or seven quarts of water, although some say a gallon (4 quarts) is ample for a pound of pasta. We suggest you bring a large pot of water to the boil, add salt (about a tablespoon for every three or four quarts) and immediately plunge the pasta into the water. Cook it over high heat so that the water quickly returns to the boil and the pasta cooks rapidly. Depending on the size and shape of the pasta, as well as whether it is dried or fresh, the pasta will take from one or two to 10 minutes to cook. The times we give in our recipes are gauged for dry pasta. *Never* break strands of pasta before putting them in the pot—unless a recipe specifies that you do so. If the pot is too small, let the ends of the strands cook for a minute or so before pushing the rest into the pot. We are not sure why, we admit, but unbroken pasta tastes better and holds the sauce more satisfactorily.

Stir the pasta only a little as it cooks, and never use a spoon. A spoon tends to gather the strands or shapes together. A wooden pasta fork does the best job of separating the strands as they cook. Our recipes call for the pasta to be cooked until al dente, which means it should have a little "bite" when you test it between your teeth. Depend more on this test than on time to determine when the pasta is done. Lift the pasta from the pot with the fork and let it drain back into the water or, more conveniently, drain the cooked noodles in a colander. Do not rinse them—you will wash away their good flavor.

Pasta should be eaten as soon as it is cooked, unless it is for a casserole or cold salad. Transfer the drained pasta to a warm bowl or individual plates and spoon sauce over it at once. Now that's a meal!

PASTA GLOSSARY

STRAND PASTAS:

capellini—the very thinnest round strand pasta
fidelini—nearly as thin as capellini
vermicelli—thinner than spaghetti
spaghetti—thin, round strand pasta
fusilli—thin, twisted strand pasta
linguine—flat, narrow strand pasta
fettuccine—flat strand pasta, wider than linguine
lasagne—wide, flat pasta

PASTA SHAPES:

orzo—tiny, grain-like pasta
pastina—translates to "tiny dough" and is a very small pasta
usually used for soup
ditalini—small, short macaroni
macaroni—a general term for hollow pasta
penne/mostaccioli—grooved or straight sided tubes also called
moustaches
rotelle—corkscrew-shaped pasta
ziti—large tubular macaroni
rigatoni—large tubular macaroni with grooved sides
shells—shell-shaped pasta of varying sizes
elbows—hollow tubes of pasta bent into semicircles
farfalle/butterflies/bow ties—shaped like bow ties or butterflies
tortellini—filled twists of pasta
ravioli—filled squares of pasta
manicotti—large straight-ended tubes for stuffing
cannelloni—large tubes for stuffing with the ends cut on the
diagonal; sometimes with grooved sides

CHAPTER 1

PASTA BASICS

A platter of steaming hot pasta, smothered with a dark red sauce, has become an all-American meal. Everyone loves it, from the toddler in the high chair (with the sauce all over his face!) to the oldest, most dignified member of the family. Tell your kids you are planning spaghetti with meat sauce, a green salad and a loaf of garlic bread for supper and you won't have any trouble keeping them home for the evening meal.

Here, we have grouped what we consider the "basic" pasta sauces along with a basic recipe for fresh egg pasta. The sauces go splendidly with fresh or packaged pasta. You will find a meatless red sauce, a traditional meat sauce, a fresh tomato sauce, a spicy anchovy sauce and bright green pesto. Master these and you will never again open a jar of spaghetti sauce from the supermarket. The red sauces and the pesto freeze well—make large batches and stow them away in containers that hold four to six cups. Thaw the sauce overnight in the refrigerator or quickly in the microwave. Pasta takes only minutes to cook. Presto!—a wholesome meal that everyone adores.

Homemade Egg Pasta

Makes about 1 pound; serves 4

Making your own pasta is fast and easy when you have a food processor and can roll it and cut it with a manual pasta machine. We do not recommend making it by hand, unaided by these invaluable devices, when so much excellent, fresh pasta is widely available in the markets.

1½ - 1¾ cups all-purpose flour
3 large eggs
2 teaspoons olive oil

For spinach pasta, add 2 tablespoons drained, chopped frozen spinach and 2 additional tablespoons of flour to the workbowl of the food processor. Then proceed with the recipe.

Put 1½ cups of the flour in the workbowl of a food processor along with the eggs and the olive oil. Process for about 30 seconds. If the mixture forms a ball immediately and is wet to the touch, mix in the remaining flour by the tablespoon and process until the dough feels soft but not sticky.

Divide the dough into quarters. Flatten one of these to about a ½-inch thickness and lightly flour both sides. With the pasta machine's smooth rollers adjusted to the widest setting, pass the dough through the feeder. Fold into thirds, flatten it, and run it through this setting 5 more times to knead the dough. The kneaded dough should be smooth and satiny.

Adjust the control to the next smallest setting, and feed the sheet through the machine. Do not fold at this point. Repeat the process, narrowing the setting each time, until the desired thickness is achieved—usually with the next-to-last setting. Flour the dough as necessary to prevent sticking. Lay the sheet on a lightly floured surface and repeat with the remaining portions of dough. With a knife, cut the sheets in half crosswise for easier handling.

To cut the noodles, run one piece of dough at a time

through the selected cutting rollers. Gently toss the noodles with flour and set them aside on a baking sheet. The pasta may be cooked immediately or left to dry uncovered for 2 to 3 hours.

Basic Tomato Sauce

Makes about 6 cups; serves 6

The vegetables make this meatless sauce a little chunky and deliciously flavorful. Spoon it over almost any shape of pasta.

> $1/4$ cup olive oil
> 1 onion, chopped
> 1 carrot, chopped
> 1 stalk celery, chopped
> 1 small green pepper, chopped
> 1 clove garlic, finely chopped
> 28-ounce can crushed tomatoes in puree
> 16-ounce can tomato sauce
> $1/4$ cup red wine or water
> $1/4$ cup water
> 1 teaspoon dried oregano
> $3/4$ teaspoon dried basil
> $3/4$ teaspoon salt
> $1/4$ teaspoon pepper

Heat the oil in a large saucepan and cook the onion, carrot, celery and green pepper over medium-low heat for about 5 minutes until just softened. Add the garlic and cook for 1 minute. Add the crushed tomatoes, tomato sauce, wine, water, oregano, basil, salt and pepper. Cook gently over low heat, uncovered, for 30 minutes. Taste and add salt and pepper if needed.

It's a fair estimate to allow 1 pound of pasta for 4 adults. Children, of course, love pasta, so perhaps you should figure that 1 pound serves 4 people—big or small—*period*.

Basic Meat Sauce

Makes about 7 cups

Enough for one pound of pasta, which easily serves four adults, this rich, meaty sauce is what most folks think of when they ask for "meat sauce." Spoon it over all but the most delicate pastas.

Making your own sauce is nutritious—prepared sauces are high in sodium, fat and sugar (corn syrup, usually).

2 tablespoons olive oil
1 pound ground beef
1 large onion, chopped
2 cloves garlic, finely chopped
28-ounce can crushed plum tomatoes in puree
6-ounce can tomato paste
2 cups water
2 teaspoons dried basil
1 bay leaf, broken in half
1 teaspoon sugar
3/4 teaspoon salt
1/2 teaspoon pepper

Heat the olive oil in a large, heavy pot. Add the ground beef and onion and cook over moderate heat, stirring frequently, for about 10 minutes until the meat has lost its pink color. Add the garlic and cook for 1 minute.

Stir in all the remaining ingredients, bring to the boil, reduce the heat to very low and cook gently, uncovered, for 30 minutes until the sauce is quite thick. If the sauce is too thick, stir in 1/2 cup of water or more.

Taste for seasoning and add more salt and pepper, if needed. This will depend on the saltiness of the tomatoes and tomato paste. The sauce can be refrigerated for up to 4 days and freezes very well.

Pesto Sauce

Makes about 1¼ cups; serves 6

There is good reason why this sauce has gained such a stellar reputation. The combination of fresh basil leaves, pungent garlic, pine nuts and heady, golden-green olive oil is hard to beat. Make a lot of the sauce in the summer and freeze it for those cold winter days when you want a taste of August. It also adds bright flavor spooned into hot vegetable soup. This recipe makes enough pesto for a pound of pasta and we recommend it tossed with linguine, capellini or meat or cheese tortellini.

> *2 cups packed fresh basil leaves*
> *2 large cloves garlic*
> *4 tablespoons pine nuts*
> *¼ teaspoon salt*
> *½ cup olive oil*
> *½ cup (2 ounces) grated Parmesan cheese*
> *2 tablespoons (1 ounce) butter, softened*

Put the basil, garlic, pine nuts, salt and oil in a food processor or blender and puree until smooth. Add the cheese and butter and process a few seconds until just incorporated. Taste and add more salt if needed.

COOKING FRESH PASTA

To cook fresh pasta, bring a large pot of water to the boil. Add a good pinch of salt, and cook the pasta at a rapid boil for 1½ to 3 minutes, or until al dente. Drain in a colander and serve. Fresh pasta cooks more quickly than dry because it already contains a good amount of moisture.

Fresh Tomato and Basil Sauce

Makes 4 to 5 cups; serves 6

When the tomatoes are bursting on the vines in late summer and fresh basil is widely available, try this light, fresh-tasting sauce over spaghetti, capellini, linguine or other thin-stranded pasta. A light coating of sauce is all you need and it is so easy and quick to cook that you will be tempted to make it more than once or twice a week while the tomatoes are good.

> *5 tablespoons (2 1/2 ounces) butter*
> *3 tablespoons olive oil*
> *1/2 cup finely chopped onion*
> *3 tablespoons red wine vinegar*
> *3 1/2 pounds firm ripe tomatoes, peeled, seeded*
> *   and coarsely chopped*
> *1/3 cup packed slivered fresh basil leaves*
> *   or 4 teaspoons dried*
> *3/4 teaspoon salt*
> *1/2 teaspoon pepper*
> *Grated Parmesan cheese*

Heat the butter and oil in a large skillet. Add the onion and cook over medium-low heat for about 5 minutes until just softened. Add the vinegar and cook over moderate heat for 2 minutes. Add the tomatoes and cook gently over medium-low heat for about 15 minutes until about half of the tomato liquid is evaporated and the sauce is somewhat thickened.

Add the basil, salt and pepper and cook gently for 2 minutes more. The sauce should be served hot or warm over freshly cooked pasta. Pass the Parmesan at the table.

Anchovy Sauce

Makes about 1 cup

If you like the salty bite of anchovies, this sauce is custom-made for you. It is especially good with thin spaghetti and vermicelli; the recipe makes enough for a pound of pasta.

> *½ cup olive oil*
> *6 tablespoons (3 ounces) butter*
> *2 cloves garlic, finely chopped*
> *12 anchovies, chopped, with their oil*
> *½ teaspoon pepper*
> *¼ cup finely chopped parsley*

Combine the oil, butter, garlic, anchovies and pepper in a saucepan. Cook gently over low heat for about 3 minutes. Add the parsley and cook for 1 minute. The sauce may be made ahead and refrigerated for up to 2 days.

TOMATO TIPS

When you pick or buy vine-ripened tomatoes, do not be put off by any that are yellow around the stem end. This is how they ripen naturally. Choose fruit that feels firm, heavy and a little soft, with good, deep red color. Once you have selected them, never refrigerate tomatoes. Set them on the kitchen shelf or sill.

During those drab months when tomatoes are not wonderful, use the best plum tomatoes you can find—no need to skin them if you chop them fine.

CHAPTER 2

PASTA CLASSICS

Our love for all things prepared with pasta has turned a number of pasta dishes into American classics. Some, such as Fettuccine Alfredo and Pasta Puttanesca, are considered classics in Italy, too. Cincinnati-Style Chili, by contrast, is a stateside invention that earned its classic designation by its quick popularity. Whatever your definition of a classic pasta dish, the recipes in this chapter will surely become traditions in your household.

The recipes are all for stranded pastas—in other words, none are for shell or tubular shapes. Strands of pasta take well to smooth sauces, and, as a rule, the thinner the sauce, the thinner the pasta strand ought to be. Thick creamy Alfredo sauce does better on flat fettuccine than on skinny, rounded vermicelli. In fact, some purists feel Fettuccine Alfredo should be made only with homemade pasta, because the soft, moist noodles will absorb the sauce to produce a flavor and texture not achievable with packaged pasta. Chunky Carbonara sauce, however, tastes best when tossed with sturdy, thick spaghetti. Follow our recommendations for the types of pasta to use with each sauce and you will not go wrong.

Spaghetti with Oil and Garlic

If you have olive oil, a head of garlic and a package of thin spaghetti or vermicelli, you can make a feast fit for a king. Fresh, firm garlic is crucial, and you really should *like* the way the olive oil tastes. Serve this as a first course or light meal—toss in a few handfuls of cooked peas, zucchini or asparagus for variety.

> 1 pound thin spaghetti
> 3/4 cup olive oil
> 2 teaspoons finely chopped garlic (3–4 cloves)
> 1/2 teaspoon salt
> 1/4 teaspoon dried red pepper flakes
> 1/4 cup finely chopped parsley

Bring a large pot of water to the boil for the pasta. Add salt and the spaghetti and boil for 6 to 8 minutes or until al dente. Drain well.

While the pasta is boiling, gently heat the olive oil, garlic, salt and red pepper flakes for about 5 minutes. Do not allow to come to the boil.

Put the pasta in a large warm serving dish and pour the oil over it. Add the parsley. Toss gently but thoroughly to coat all of the pasta.

OLIVE OIL

Virgin and extra-virgin olive oils cost more because they are made from the first pressing of the olives, while less expensive oils, which lack the rich flavor of virgin oils, are generally made from a second or even third pressing. Good olive oil usually has a deep greenish tint and is worth the investment when it plays an assertive role.

Spaghetti and Meatballs

Serves 6

Here is a classic pasta dish—at least in the United States. And the sauce tastes great when made a day or two in advance and reheated just before serving. Simmered in the sauce, the meatballs give it richness and do not need to be browned. The pork and veal provide good flavor, but you may opt to use ground beef only.

SAUCE:
3 tablespoons olive oil
1 large onion, chopped
2 cloves garlic, finely chopped
28-ounce can crushed tomatoes in puree
2 16-ounce cans tomato sauce
1 teaspoon sugar
1 teaspoon dried oregano
3/4 teaspoon salt
1/2 teaspoon pepper
1 bay leaf, broken in half

MEATBALLS:
1 pound lean ground chuck
1/4 pound ground veal
1/4 pound ground pork
1 large egg
1/2 cup fresh bread crumbs
2 tablespoons grated Parmesan cheese
2 tablespoons finely chopped parsley
1 teaspoon dried basil
1/2 teaspoon salt
1/4 teaspoon pepper
1 pound spaghetti
Grated Parmesan cheese

To make the sauce, heat the oil in a large saucepan and cook the onion over medium-low heat for about 5 minutes until just softened. Add the garlic and cook 1 minute. Add the crushed tomatoes, tomato sauce, sugar, oregano, salt, pepper and bay leaf. Cook gently over low heat, uncovered, for 15 minutes.

While the sauce is cooking, make the meatballs. Use your hands to combine the ground chuck, veal, pork, egg, bread crumbs, cheese, parsley, basil, salt and pepper in a large mixing bowl. Form into about 18 meatballs, each about 1½ inches in diameter.

Put the meatballs into the simmering sauce, arranging them close together. Spoon some sauce over the tops of the meatballs if they are not completely submerged, but take care not to break them up with the spoon.

Partially cover the pan and cook gently over low heat for 20 minutes until the meatballs are just firm. Stir gently, then continue to cook, partially covered, for about 15 minutes until the meatballs are cooked through. Remove and discard the bay leaf pieces. Spoon off any excess fat that rises to the surface of the sauce.

Bring a large pot of water to the boil for the pasta. Add salt and the spaghetti and boil for 9 minutes or until al dente. Drain well. Serve the pasta with the sauce and meatballs spooned over. Pass the Parmesan at the table.

Cooking pasta "al dente" means cooking it until it is just done and still firm. The term translates, roughly, as "to the tooth"—which means you should be able to feel the pasta when you bite it. It should not be overly soft. Al dente pasta is generally tossed with hot sauce, which cooks it a little more, too.

Pasta Puttanesca

Serves 6

A lusty and forthright blending of ingredients named for Italian ladies of the night (the *puttane*), tasty Puttanesca sauce should be used rather sparingly. Two-thirds of a cup is about right for a serving of pasta.

1/4 cup olive oil
3 cloves garlic, finely chopped
2 28-ounce cans plum tomatoes, drained
3/4 cup sliced or chopped black olives
6 anchovy fillets
2 tablespoons drained capers
1/2 cup chopped parsley, preferably Italian
flat-leaf
1 teaspoon dried oregano
1/2 teaspoon dried red pepper flakes
1 pound linguine or spaghetti
Grated Parmesan cheese

Parmesan and Romano cheese are very dry and very hard because they are aged for many months. The best should be aged for at least two years.

Heat the oil in a large skillet. Add the garlic and cook over moderate heat for 1 minute. Add the drained tomatoes, breaking them up with the side of a spoon. Stir in the olives, anchovies and capers. Bring to the boil, lower the heat and cook gently, uncovered, for 15 to 20 minutes until the sauce is quite thick. Stir in the parsley, oregano and red pepper flakes and cook gently for another 5 minutes. The sauce may be made ahead and stored in the refrigerator for up to two days. Reheat before serving.

Bring a large pot of water to the boil for the pasta. Add salt and cook the pasta at a rapid boil for about 9 minutes until al dente. Drain in a colander and transfer to a serving platter or individual plates. Spoon the hot sauce over the pasta and serve, sprinkled generously with Parmesan cheese.

Fettuccine Alfredo

Serves 6 as a main course; 6 to 8 as a first course

A wonderfully rich and creamy classic, this makes a good first course for an Italian meal. It is also a satisfying main course; serve it with sliced ham and a green salad.

> *1 pound fettuccine*
> *8 tablespoons (4 ounces) butter, melted*
> *1 cup (4 ounces) grated Parmesan cheese*
> *3/4 cup heavy cream*
> *3/4 teaspoon salt*
> *1/2 teaspoon black pepper*
> *Pinch of ground nutmeg*

Bring a large pot of water to the boil for the pasta. Add salt and the fettuccine and cook at a rapid boil for about 9 minutes until al dente.

Drain the pasta in a colander and return it to the still-warm cooking pot. Pour the melted butter over the fettuccine and toss with two large spoons until the strands are coated. Sprinkle on the Parmesan, pour in the cream and toss again until the pasta is coated with the smooth, creamy sauce. Season with the salt, pepper and nutmeg, and taste for seasoning. The dish may need more salt, depending on the saltiness of the Parmesan. Serve on warm plates.

NOTE: An alternative method is to heat a large serving bowl in a warm oven while the pasta is cooking. Put the drained fettuccine in the warm bowl and toss with the remaining ingredients.

According to Craig Claiborne, the word spaghetti derives from the Italian term *spago*, which means "string." Fettuccine means "small ribbons" and vermicelli means "little worms."

Cincinnati-Style Chili

Serves 6

Why this slightly spicy dish is a tradition in Cincinnati remains somewhat of a mystery—but we're glad it is. Don't be put off by the number of ingredients. Like other styles of chili, this one is easy to throw together. Put all the fixings, including a bowl of just-cooked spaghetti, on a buffet table and let your family and guests go wild. They will certainly be back for seconds. Remember that true Cincinnati Chili is always topped with cheddar cheese, onions, or kidney beans—or all three.

2 pounds ground chuck
1 large onion, finely chopped
3 cloves garlic, finely chopped
3 tablespoons chili powder
2 teaspoons paprika
1 teaspoon cumin
1 teaspoon dried oregano
3/4 teaspoon salt
1/4 teaspoon cayenne pepper
1/4 teaspoon cinnamon
1/8 teaspoon ground cloves
16-ounce can tomato sauce
1 1/4 cups water
1/4 cup cider vinegar
1 tablespoon Worcestershire sauce
1/2 ounce unsweetened chocolate
1 pound spaghetti
*Grated cheddar cheese, chopped onion and
    cooked pinto beans (optional)*

In a large saucepan, cook the beef with the onion and garlic over medium-low heat for about 10 minutes until the meat has lost its red color. Drain off any excess fat.

Stir in the chili powder, paprika, cumin, oregano, salt, cayenne, cinnamon and cloves and cook for 1 minute over moderate heat, stirring often. Add the the tomato sauce, water, vinegar, Worcestershire and chocolate.

Cover and cook gently for 1 hour, stirring frequently. Uncover and cook for about 15 minutes, stirring often, until thickened. The recipe can be made two days ahead to this point.

When ready to serve the chili, bring a large pot of water to the boil for the pasta. Add salt and the spaghetti and cook for about 9 minutes or until al dente. Drain well.

Serve the chili spooned over the pasta in a large shallow platter or on individual plates. Serve the cheese, onion and/or beans separately for each guest to add to the chili as desired.

Spaghetti Carbonara

Serves 4 to 6

In Italy, this easy, filling pasta dish is made for quick suppers and lunches. Because it utilizes what every housewife has on hand—pasta, eggs, cheese and bacon—it is never considered fussy or fancy. Indeed, it should not be. It is simply very, very good.

> 1 pound thick spaghetti (percatelli) or regular spaghetti
> 3/4 pound bacon, preferably thick-sliced, cut into 3/4-inch pieces
> 2 tablespoons bacon drippings
> 3 eggs
> 1/2 cup (2 ounces) grated Parmesan cheese
> 1/4 cup finely chopped parsley
> 3/4 teaspoon coarsely ground black pepper
> 1/2 teaspoon salt

For maximum flavor, cheese should always be freshly grated.

Bring a large pot of water to the boil for the pasta. Add salt and cook the spaghetti at a rapid boil for about 9 minutes until al dente.

Meanwhile, cook the bacon in a large skillet over moderate heat until crisp, separating the pieces as they cook. Remove with a slotted spoon and drain on paper towels. Reserve 2 tablespoons of the drippings.

In a small bowl, whisk together the bacon drippings, eggs, cheese, parsley, pepper and salt.

When the pasta is cooked, drain in a colander and return to the still-warm pot. Pour the egg/cheese mixture over the hot spaghetti and toss with two large spoons until the pasta is well coated with sauce. The residual heat will cook the egg slightly. Add the bacon, toss again and serve on warm plates.

CHAPTER 3

PASTA SOUPS

A bowl of piping hot, homemade soup on the table is always welcome, whether it is for a weekday meal, Saturday-night supper or a casual Sunday lunch. Serving soup says you care and shows you want to feed your family and good friends in the most warming, comforting, nutritious way you know how. Usually all you need to go with a good soup is a loaf of bread—buy one, freshly baked, from a local bakery or specialty shop—and a green salad. A glass of wine tastes good, too.

Soup is a joy to make. Measurements need not be precise, so if, for instance, you prefer a little more chicken in your chicken noodle soup, add another half cup or so. If you like your minestrone without tomatoes, leave them out. Soup also benefits from being made ahead of time and being reheated just before serving. As with stews, the extra time gives the flavors and ingredients time to develop so that the soup is as tasty as can be. And soup makes great leftovers—just right for a late-night snack or lunch the next day. So, when the fall winds blow, the winter snows drift or the spring rains fall, it's time to move into the kitchen and make a big pot of soup.

27

Pastina in Broth

Serves 6

Few soups are easier to make than this one. If you have homemade chicken broth on hand, all the better. Pastina, the tiniest of pastas, is a great favorite with children. Give yours this soup on a cold, windy evening, or pack it in their lunch-box thermos for a comforting taste of home during the school day.

Cook pastina in boiling water, drain and toss it with butter and a little salt. It makes a soothing and tasty side dish. Children love it.

> 12 cups chicken broth
> 3 carrots, peeled and sliced into very thin rounds
> 3 ounces (1 cup) pastina
> 1 tablespoon finely chopped parsley
> 1 tablespoon finely chopped marjoram or thyme or 1 teaspoon dried
> 1/2 cup (2 ounces) grated Parmesan cheese

Put the chicken broth in a large saucepan or soup pot. Add the carrots and bring to the boil. Cook, covered, over low heat for 6 minutes. Add the pastina and continue to cook over low heat for about 4 minutes until the pasta is cooked.

Stir in the parsley and marjoram and ladle the soup into bowls. Sprinkle generously with Parmesan and pass the remaining cheese at the table.

PUTTING PASTA IN SOUP

Remember that pasta tends to get soggy if allowed to overcook in the soup's broth, so you might choose to wait until you are reheating the soup to add the pasta. It absorbs the flavor of the soup, so check the seasonings before serving.

Alphabet Soup

Serves 6 (about 10 cups)

While any small pasta, such as tubettini, ditalini, farfalle or elbow macaroni, can be added to this filling,
meaty soup, alphabet macaroni makes it fun.

> 2 tablespoons vegetable oil
> 1 1/2 pounds beef chuck, cut in 3/4-inch cubes
> 1 large onion, chopped
> 1 clove garlic, finely chopped
> 28-ounce can tomatoes and their juice
> 2 cups beef broth
> 3 cups water
> 1 teaspoon dried marjoram
> 1 teaspoon dried thyme
> 1 teaspoon dried savory
> 1/2 teaspoon pepper
> 10-ounce package frozen mixed vegetables
> 1/3 cup alphabet macaroni
> 4 tablespoons finely chopped parsley

Heat the oil in a large (5-quart) soup pot or kettle.
Cook the beef in the oil, a third at a time, over medium-
high heat until browned. As each batch of meat browns,
remove it from the pan with a slotted spoon. After all
of the meat has browned, add the onion and garlic to
the drippings in the pot and cook over medium-low
heat for 5 minutes until the onions are just softened.

Return the meat to the pot and add the tomatoes,
broth, water, marjoram, thyme, savory and pepper.
Cook gently, partially covered, for 45 minutes. Add the
vegetables and macaroni and cook over moderate heat
for 10 to 12 minutes until the pasta is al dente. Stir in
the parsley, and add salt and pepper if needed.

*Stelline, orzo,
anellini, nocchette
and conchigliette
are all tiny,
traditional soup
pastas.*

Old-Fashioned Chicken Noodle Soup

Serves 6 (about 14 cups)

Once upon a time, country kitchens from Pennsylvania to Idaho boasted big pots of chicken noodle soup gently cooking on dark, iron cookstoves. The wide egg noodles and easy seasonings blend happily with the tender chunks of chicken to make a soup that warms the soul as well as the body and speaks to us of all the good things about going home.

Chicken broth, easy to make in quantity, freezes very well. Keep several containers of it in the freezer so that you can make soup any time. Canned broth is good, too.

3- to 3 1/2-pound chicken, cut in 6 or 8 pieces
6 cups chicken broth
6 cups water
1 large onion, chopped
2 stalks celery, thinly sliced
1 bay leaf, broken in half
1 1/2 teaspoons dried thyme
1 teaspoon poultry seasoning
3 ounces egg noodles
10-ounce package frozen peas and carrots
3/4 teaspoon salt
1/4 teaspoon pepper

Put the chicken in a large soup pot along with the chicken broth and water. Bring to the boil over high heat, reduce the heat to moderate and cook, uncovered, for 10 minutes, skimming off any foam and fat that rises to the surface.

Add the onion, celery and bay leaf and cook, partially covered, over low heat for 30 minutes until the chicken is tender and no longer pink.

Remove the chicken from the pot with tongs and set it aside until it is cool enough to handle. Spoon off as much of the fat from the surface of the soup as possible.

Add the thyme, poultry seasoning, noodles, peas and carrots, salt and pepper to the pot. Cook gently, partially covered, for about 8 minutes.

Meanwhile, remove the skin from the chicken, take the meat off the bones and cut it into ¾-inch chunks. You should have about 3 cups. Return the meat to the soup and heat through. Taste for seasoning and serve.

Pasta and Bean Soup

Serves 6 (about 12 cups)

Here is a wholesome and robust soup that is best ladled into wide bowls and flavored with a generous sprinkling of Parmesan cheese. The bean-pasta-cheese combination provides complete protein without any meat.

⅓ cup olive oil
1 large onion, chopped
3 carrots, peeled and thinly sliced
2 stalks celery, thinly sliced
2 cloves garlic, finely chopped
2 1-pound cans kidney beans and their liquid
1-pound can tomatoes and their juice
2 cups beef broth
5 cups water
3 ounces (1 cup) tubetti
1 teaspoon dried rosemary
½ teaspoon dried oregano
¾ teaspoon salt
¼ teaspoon pepper
½ cup chopped parsley
Grated Parmesan cheese

A soup pot should be heavy and deep. The heaviness prevents the soup from burning on the bottom during long simmering; the deepness prevents too much liquid from evaporating during heating and reheating.

(continued)

Heat the olive oil in a large soup pot. Add the onion, carrots, celery and garlic and cook over low heat for 10 minutes until softened.

Stir in the beans and the tomatoes, breaking up the tomatoes with a spoon. Add the beef broth and water and bring to the boil over high heat. Add the pasta and the rosemary, oregano, salt and pepper. Lower the heat and cook gently, partially covered, for 15 to 20 minutes until the pasta is cooked. Stir in the parsley. Taste for seasoning, adding more salt and pepper if needed. Keep in mind that the Parmesan will add some saltiness, so do not oversalt. Ladle into bowls and sprinkle each serving with a generous spoonful of Parmesan.

Minestrone

Serves 6 (about 11 cups)

In nearly every Italian kitchen, at one time or another, a pot of minestrone simmers on the back burner of the stove. Everyone who passes by tosses a few vegetables, some fresh herbs or other seasoning into the pot. Beans and pasta are always included; meat never is.

> 1/4 cup olive oil
> 1 large onion, chopped
> 1 clove garlic, finely chopped
> 1 stalk celery, sliced
> 1 large carrot, sliced
> 16-ounce can tomatoes and their juice
> 4 cups beef broth
> 1 1/2 cups water
> 1 1/2 teaspoons dried thyme

1 ½ teaspoons dried basil
½ teaspoon pepper
1 large potato (8 ounces), cut in ½-inch cubes
½ cup elbow macaroni
2 cups thinly sliced cabbage
1 zucchini, sliced
16-ounce can white cannellini beans, undrained
4 tablespoons grated Parmesan cheese

Heat the oil in a large (5-quart) soup pot or kettle. Cook the onion, garlic, celery and carrot in the oil for about 5 minutes over medium-low heat until the vegetables begin to soften. Add the tomatoes with their liquid, broth, water, thyme, basil and pepper and bring just to the boil.

Add the potato and macaroni and cook, uncovered, over moderate heat for 10 minutes. Add the cabbage, zucchini and beans with their liquid and cook for 10 minutes. Stir in the Parmesan. Taste and add salt if needed.

Heat up a mug or bowl of leftover soup in the microwave for a quick and nutritious snack.

CHAPTER 4

PASTA CASSEROLES

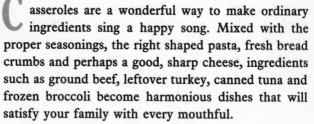

Casseroles are a wonderful way to make ordinary ingredients sing a happy song. Mixed with the proper seasonings, the right shaped pasta, fresh bread crumbs and perhaps a good, sharp cheese, ingredients such as ground beef, leftover turkey, canned tuna and frozen broccoli become harmonious dishes that will satisfy your family with every mouthful.

Casseroles do much more, too, than taste good. They simplify a busy life. Whether refrigerated for a day or frozen for a month, they are admirable time-savers during that hectic hour just before dinner—put them in the oven and let them heat through, no stirring, no fussing. Some cooks prefer to buy a lot of ingredients at one time and make several casseroles during the weekend. This way they have them on hand in the freezer for the month to come. Because it is practical to make casseroles in fairly large quantities, today's small families benefit from the leftovers, which can be reheated in a microwave or more conventionally in the oven. The rich blending of flavors in any casserole keeps the palate alert for two or even three consecutive meals.

Chicken Divan and Pasta Casserole

Serves 6

This creamy casserole is reminiscent of Chicken Divan, the standby buffet party dish of the 1950s and 1960s, but tastier, more contemporary. It has the requisite broccoli and cheese sauce—both delicious—but because it is made with pasta, three kinds of cheese and fresh bread crumbs, its flavor and texture are decidedly lively. The shells are pretty, but substitute bow ties or butterfly pasta (called farfalle) for a different look. Serve this with a tossed green salad, broiled tomato halves and French bread.

10 ounces small or medium-sized pasta shells
4 cups broccoli florets (about 1 pound)
4 tablespoons (2 ounces) butter
1 onion, chopped
1/2 small red bell pepper, chopped
1 tablespoon all-purpose flour
1 cup heavy cream
1/3 cup milk
2/3 cup white wine
1 cup (4 ounces) ricotta cheese
1 cup (4 ounces) grated cheddar cheese
2/3 cup grated Parmesan cheese
1 pound cooked chicken or turkey, cut in
*   3/4-inch pieces*
1/2 cup fresh bread crumbs

Make fresh bread crumbs by cubing several slices of bread, after trimming the crusts. Put the cubes in a blender or food processor and process until the bread is the consistency you prefer. One slice makes about a half cup. Fresh crumbs keep very well in the refrigerator in a lidded glass jar.

Bring a large pot of water to the boil for the pasta. Add salt and the shells and boil for 6 minutes. Add the broccoli to the pasta and boil an additional 2 to 3 minutes until the pasta is al dente and the broccoli is crisp-tender. Drain well and return the pasta and broccoli to the cooking pot.

Meanwhile, heat the butter in a large skillet and cook the onion and red pepper over medium-low heat for 5 minutes until they are just softened. Stir in the flour and cook, stirring, for 1 minute. Stir in the cream, milk and wine and bring just to the boil, stirring constantly. Stir in the ricotta and remove the skillet from the heat. Stir in the cheddar and ⅓ cup of the Parmesan until the cheeses are melted and well blended. Add the sauce and the chicken to the pasta and broccoli and mix gently.

Spoon the pasta mixture into a buttered 9-by-13-inch pan. Combine the bread crumbs with the remaining Parmesan and sprinkle the mixture evenly over the casserole.

Heat the oven to 350 degrees.

Bake for 20 to 25 minutes until the casserole is heated through and the bread crumbs are golden.

Tex-Mex Spaghetti Pie

Serves 6

This very untraditional pie, with baked spaghetti as the "crust," will become a favorite in any household, particularly those with children. It combines the sunny flavors of the Southwest with the pleasing texture of pasta. For a spicier filling, use a hot Italian sausage in place of some of the ground beef.

> *8 ounces spaghetti*
> *⅓ cup milk*
> *1 large egg*

1 pound ground chuck
1 onion, chopped
1 green pepper, chopped
4-ounce can chopped green chilies
1 tablespoon chili powder
3/4 teaspoon cumin
1/2 teaspoon dried oregano
1/2 teaspoon salt
1/4 teaspoon cayenne pepper
16-ounce can tomato sauce
2 cups (8 ounces) grated Monterey jack cheese

Bring a large pot of water to the boil for the pasta. Add salt and the spaghetti and boil for about 9 minutes or until al dente. Drain well. Beat the milk with the egg and toss with the hot pasta until well blended. Arrange the pasta in a buttered 9-by-13-inch pan to make an even bed, or "crust."

Cook the ground chuck in a large skillet over moderate heat until it loses most of its color. Add the onion and green pepper and cook for about 5 minutes over medium-low heat until the vegetables are just softened. Stir in the chilies, chili powder, cumin, oregano, salt and cayenne, then stir in the tomato sauce. Cook gently, uncovered, over low heat for about 5 minutes.

Spoon the meat evenly over the pasta in the pan. Sprinkle the meat with the cheese.

Heat the oven to 350 degrees.

Bake for 20 to 25 minutes until the casserole is heated through and the cheese is melted. Let the casserole stand for 5 minutes, then cut it into squares and serve.

Spinach Lasagne

Serves 8

Traditional lasagne is made with a cream sauce rather than a tomato sauce. This robust, creamy casserole draws on that tradition and includes a tasty spinach-based filling made with ground turkey, now widely available in most supermarkets.

FILLING:
2 tablespoons vegetable oil
1 pound ground turkey or veal
1 medium-size onion, chopped
1 clove garlic, finely chopped
1/2 cup white wine
*10-ounce box frozen chopped spinach, thawed
    and drained*
2 teaspoons dried basil or mixed herbs
1/2 teaspoon salt
1/8 teaspoon black pepper

SAUCE:
4 tablespoons (2 ounces) butter
4 tablespoons all-purpose flour
1 1/2 cups chicken broth
1 1/2 cups milk
1/2 teaspoon salt
1/8 teaspoon pepper
1/4 teaspoon ground nutmeg

*12 ounces spinach or egg lasagne noodles (about
    12 standard-sized noodles)*
1 cup (4 ounces) ricotta cheese
3 cups (12 ounces) grated mozzarella cheese
1/4 cup (1 ounce) grated Parmesan cheese

Lasagne noodles may be straight-edged or curly. Spinach lasagne is also called *lasagne verde.*

To make the filling, heat the oil in a large skillet. Add the turkey and onion and cook over moderate heat for about 8 minutes until the meat loses its pink color. Add the garlic and continue to cook for about 2 minutes until the meat is cooked through and the onion is softened. Spoon off any excess fat. Add the wine to the skillet and cook over high heat until most of the liquid has evaporated. Add the drained spinach and season the mixture with the basil, salt and pepper. Set the filling aside.

To make the sauce, heat the butter in a moderate saucepan. Stir in the flour and cook, stirring, over moderate heat for 2 minutes. Gradually whisk in the chicken broth and milk. Bring to the boil, reduce the heat to moderate and cook, stirring, for 1 minute until smooth and thickened. Season with salt, pepper and nutmeg.

Bring a large pot of water to the boil for the pasta. Add salt and cook the lasagne noodles at a rapid boil for about 10 minutes until al dente. Drain in a colander, refresh under cold water and drain again.

Lightly butter a 9-by-13-inch pan. Spoon a little of the sauce into the pan, tilting it to coat the bottom. Begin the layering, first with three or four of the lasagne noodles, then with half the meat-spinach mixture. Dot with half the ricotta and about a third of the mozzarella. Repeat the process with a second layer. The top should be a layer of noodles, the last of the sauce and a sprinkling of the last of the mozzarella and the Parmesan.

Heat the oven to 375 degrees.

Bake the lasagne uncovered for 30 to 45 minutes until it is heated all the way through and the top is glazed a light brown. Serve cut into wedges.

Pack a square of lasagne or macaroni and cheese in a plastic container and tote it to work. Keep it in the office refrigerator and then heat it up in the microwave for lunch.

Turkey Tetrazzini

Serves 6

Long a favorite way to use leftover turkey or chicken, tetrazzini can be "modernized" in a flash by using a mixture of wild mushrooms (shiitake, oyster, morels). Even made with domestic white mushrooms, it is a rich and delicious casserole, fit for company any night of the week.

VEGETABLE–MEAT MIXTURE:

2 tablespoons (1 ounce) butter
4 ounces mushrooms (any kind), sliced (about 2 cups)
1 stalk celery, thinly sliced
1 red bell pepper, cut into 1/4-inch slices
2 1/2 cups cooked turkey or chicken, cut into 3/4-inch pieces (about 1 pound)

SAUCE:

3 tablespoons (1 1/2 ounces) butter
2 tablespoons finely chopped shallots or scallions
3 tablespoons all-purpose flour
2 cups chicken broth
1/2 cup light cream or half-and-half
2 tablespoons sherry
1 teaspoon tarragon
1 teaspoon salt
1/4 teaspoon pepper
1/4 teaspoon Tabasco sauce
1/8 teaspoon ground nutmeg

10 ounces spaghetti, broken into 3-inch lengths
1/2 cup fresh bread crumbs
2 tablespoons grated Parmesan cheese
2 tablespoons (1 ounce) butter, melted
1/4 teaspoon paprika

To make the vegetable-meat mixture, heat the butter in a large skillet. Add the mushrooms and celery and cook over medium-high heat for about 5 minutes, stirring frequently. Add the red pepper and cook for 1 minute longer. Add the turkey to the skillet and set the mixture aside.

To make the sauce, heat the butter, add the chopped shallots and cook for 1 minute over moderate heat. Stir in the flour and cook, stirring, for 2 minutes. Gradually whisk in the chicken broth and light cream and bring the sauce to the boil over medium-high heat, whisking constantly. Reduce the heat to medium-low and cook, stirring, for 1 minute until the sauce is smooth and thick. Stir in the sherry and season with the tarragon, salt, pepper, Tabasco and nutmeg.

Bring a large pot of water to the boil for the pasta. Add salt and cook the noodles for about 8 minutes until al dente. Drain and refresh under cold running water.

Combine the pasta with the chicken and vegetable mixture and stir in the sauce. Transfer to a 2½- to 3-quart baking dish.

To make the crumb topping, toss the bread crumbs with the Parmesan and sprinkle the mixture evenly over the top of the casserole. Drizzle with the melted butter and sprinkle with the paprika.

Heat the oven to 375 degrees.

Bake the tetrazzini uncovered for about 35 minutes until it is nicely browned on top and bubbly around the edges. To make the top browner, put the casserole under the broiler for about 1 minute before serving.

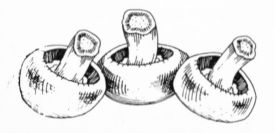

Baked Ziti

Serves 6

This is a simple way to prepare pasta and meat sauce well ahead of a meal so that when it is time for supper, you can heat the casserole and put it on the table with a green salad. It makes great leftovers, too. Don't hesitate to substitute elbows, mostaccioli or any other sturdy tubular pasta for the ziti.

Small (but not tiny) shapes are generally best in casseroles. The textured ingredients in the casserole cling to shells, bow ties and tubes.

> 8 ounces ziti
> 1 tablespoon olive oil
> ³⁄₄ pound ground beef
> 1 large onion, chopped
> 2 cloves garlic, finely chopped
> 28-ounce can crushed plum tomatoes in puree
> 16-ounce can tomato sauce
> 1 teaspoon dried oregano
> 1 teaspoon dried basil
> ¹⁄₄ teaspoon dried red pepper flakes
> 3 tablespoons chopped parsley
> Salt, if needed
> 1 cup (4 ounces) grated mozzarella cheese
> ¹⁄₄ cup (1 ounce) grated Parmesan cheese

Bring a large pot of water to the boil for the pasta. Add salt and cook the ziti at a rapid boil for about 8 minutes until al dente. Drain well.

Meanwhile, heat the olive oil in a large skillet. Add the ground beef and the onion and cook over medium-high heat, stirring and breaking up the meat with the side of a spoon, for about 8 minutes until the beef loses its color. Stir in the garlic, tomatoes, tomato sauce, oregano, basil, red pepper flakes and 2 tablespoons of the parsley. Cook gently, uncovered, over medium-low heat for about 10 minutes. Spoon off any excess fat that has risen to the surface of the sauce. (The sauce may be made ahead and stored in the refrigerator for up to 3 days.)

Either in the skillet or in the pasta pot, combine the cooked macaroni with the sauce. Taste for seasoning, adding salt if necessary. Transfer to a 2½- to 3-quart baking dish.

Toss together the mozzarella, Parmesan, and the remaining parsley in a small bowl. Sprinkle this mixture evenly over the top of the casserole.

Heat the oven to 375 degrees.

Bake the casserole uncovered for 20 to 25 minutes until the cheese is melted and flecked with brown and the sauce is bubbly around the edges.

Macaroni and Cheese

Serves 6

Here is a dish that brings back warm childhood memories—the real thing in all its creamy, crusty-topped glory—and it can easily serve as a main course for a meatless meal.

> Use elbow macaroni or a similarly sized pasta in place of the fusilli or short twists.

8 ounces fusilli or short twisted pasta
4 tablespoons (2 ounces) butter
1 small onion, finely chopped
¼ cup all-purpose flour
1 teaspoon dry mustard
2½ cups milk
3 cups (12 ounces) grated sharp cheddar cheese
¼ teaspoon pepper
¼ teaspoon Tabasco sauce

(continued)

Bring a large pot of water to the boil for the pasta. Add salt and the pasta twists and boil for about 9 minutes or until al dente. Drain well.

Meanwhile, heat the butter in a large skillet or saucepan and cook the onion for 5 minutes over medium-low heat until it is just softened. Stir in the flour and cook, stirring constantly, for 2 minutes without browning the flour. Stir in the mustard and milk and cook, stirring constantly, over moderate heat for about 3 minutes until thickened and bubbly.

Remove the skillet from the heat and add 2 cups of the cheese, ½ cup at a time, stirring until each addition is melted before adding another. Stir in the pepper and Tabasco sauce. Taste and add salt if needed.

Stir together the pasta and the sauce and spoon into a 2-quart casserole. Sprinkle the remaining cheese on top.

Heat the oven to 350 degrees.

Bake for about 15 minutes until the casserole is heated through and the cheese is melted.

NOTE: If you wish to serve the macaroni and cheese immediately without baking, stir the entire 3 cups of cheese into the hot sauce and combine with the warm pasta. Serve from a mixing bowl.

ADVANCE PREPARATION AND REHEATING

All the casseroles in this chapter can be assembled the morning before serving them, covered, and refrigerated. Or, after they are assembled, they can be wrapped well with foil and frozen for a month or two. To reheat a chilled or thawed casserole, heat it for about 20 minutes, covered with foil, at the oven temperature stated in the recipe. Uncover it and continue heating for 15 to 20 minutes longer, or until it looks the way the recipe says it should.

CHAPTER 5

STUFFED AND FILLED PASTA

Generous tubes of pasta, filled with lightly herbed, creamy cheese mixtures are the stuff that rich meals are made of. Put a platter of oversized shells, cannelloni or ravioli, covered with a smooth sauce, on the table and your guests will surely smile with contented sighs of pure pleasure. They know this meal will be completely satisfying—a richly woven fabric of texture and flavor—from the filling spooned in the softly yielding shells or tubes of pasta to the creamy, aromatic sauce.

Stuffing pasta is not as easy as simply saucing it. Several steps are necessary to prepare the finished dish. For one thing, most stuffed pastas require an accompanying sauce as well as a filling. The pasta must be cooked and cooled, the filling made and then spooned into each piece of pasta, the sauce prepared and, finally, the dish assembled. All this takes time but the final result is one of exquisite enjoyment, a labor that will please any person fortunate enough to be invited to your table.

Cheese Cannelloni with Double Mushroom Sauce

Serves 6

A heady, earthy sauce, richly imbued with wild and domestic mushrooms, turns these cheese-filled pasta tubes into a very special meal indeed. Fresh wild mushrooms, such as shiitake or morels, can be substituted for dried; you will need three ounces of fresh for the one ounce of dried. If you cannot find any sort of wild mushroom, just use a total of 11 ounces of white, domestic mushrooms. The sauce will still be delicious. Manicotti works fine if you do not have cannelloni on hand. There is very little difference.

SAUCE:
1 ounce dried mushrooms (any kind)
3 tablespoons (1 1/2 ounces) butter
1 onion, finely chopped
2 cloves garlic, finely chopped
8 ounces fresh domestic mushrooms
28-ounce can tomatoes in puree
1/2 teaspoon dried marjoram
1/2 teaspoon dried rosemary
1/4 teaspoon salt
1/8 teaspoon pepper

FILLING:
3 cups (12 ounces) ricotta cheese
6 tablespoons grated Parmesan cheese
6 tablespoons finely chopped parsley
1/4 teaspoon pepper
1 egg

8 ounces cannelloni or manicotti tubes
Grated Parmesan cheese

To make the sauce, soak the dried mushrooms in enough boiling water to cover by 1 inch for 30 minutes. Drain well, reserving the soaking liquid. Strain the liquid through cheesecloth or a coffee filter and set aside.

Heat the butter in a large skillet. Cook the onion over medium-low heat for about 3 minutes until it begins to soften. Add the garlic and fresh mushrooms and cook for about 5 minutes until the mushrooms are soft and have given up their liquid. Add the drained dried mushrooms and cook for about 2 minutes. Add the tomatoes, marjoram, rosemary, salt, pepper and ½ cup of the reserved mushroom soaking liquid. Cook gently, uncovered, for about 15 minutes adding a small amount of additional reserved liquid if the sauce becomes too thick. The sauce may be made a day ahead.

To make the filling, combine the ricotta, Parmesan, parsley, pepper and egg in a mixing bowl until well blended.

To assemble the cannelloni, bring a large pot of water to the boil for the pasta. Add salt and the cannelloni tubes and boil for 7 to 8 minutes or until al dente. Drain well and run under cool water, then drain again.

Use a small spoon to insert about 3 tablespoons of the filling into each tube. Spoon a thin layer of sauce over the bottom of a 9-by-13-inch baking dish, then lay the filled cannelloni tubes in the dish side by side and close together. Spoon the remaining sauce over the pasta and cover with foil.

Heat the oven to 350 degrees.

Bake the covered casserole for 20 to 25 minutes until heated through. Serve 2 cannelloni per person and pass the Parmesan for sprinkling on top.

NOTE: If you make the casserole early in the day and refrigerate it, heat the chilled casserole for 40 to 45 minutes at 350 degrees.

True Italian ricotta cheese, a fresh cheese in the same category as cottage cheese and pot cheese, is made from the whey of mozzarella. The ricotta available in North America is often made from the whey of cheddar or Swiss-style cheeses.

Meat Tortellini with Creamy Spinach Sauce

Serves 4 to 6

Most supermarkets carry a variety of brands of frozen tortellini and this easy and colorful sauce shows them off to their best advantage. Keep a package of tortellini in your freezer as well as an extra package of frozen spinach so that you can make this special meal anytime. Serve it with a salad of roasted red peppers and black olives, dressed with a wine vinaigrette.

To chop frozen spinach, let the package of chopped or leaf spinach thaw at room temperature or, if you are in a hurry, defrost it in the microwave. Put in a sieve and squeeze out all of the excess liquid by pressing down hard with your hands. The spinach is now ready to be chopped fine with a sharp knife or in a food processor.

3 tablespoons (1 1/2 ounces) butter
2 cloves garlic, finely chopped
3 tablespoons all-purpose flour
3 cups milk
1/4 cup white wine
1 cup thawed and drained frozen spinach, finely chopped
1 cup (4 ounces) grated Swiss cheese
1 teaspoon salt
1/4 teaspoon Tabasco sauce
1/8 teaspoon ground nutmeg
1 pound frozen meat-filled tortellini
Freshly ground black pepper

Bring a large pot of water to the boil for the tortellini. Heat the butter in a medium-large saucepan. Add the garlic and cook over low heat for 1 minute. Stir in the flour and cook, stirring over medium-high heat, for 2 minutes. Gradually whisk in the milk and the wine and bring to the boil, stirring almost constantly. Reduce the heat to moderate and cook the sauce for about 2 minutes until it is smooth and thick. Stir in the spinach and heat through. Reduce the heat to low, add the cheese and cook, stirring, until the cheese is melted. Season with the salt, Tabasco and nutmeg.

Add salt to the pasta water and cook the tortellini at a rapid boil for about 5 minutes or according to package directions until al dente. Drain well in a colander.

Reheat the sauce over low heat. Spoon the sauce over the hot tortellini and grind black pepper over the top before serving.

Lasagne Enchilada Roll-Ups

Serves 6

Bring home the flavor of sunny Mexico with this easy recipe. The "heat" can be varied by using hot, medium or mild salsa.

> *8 ounces curly lasagne noodles (about 12 noodles)*
> *15-ounce container ricotta cheese*
> *1 cup (4 ounces) grated Monterey jack cheese*
> *1 cup (4 ounces) grated sharp cheddar cheese*
> *4 tablespoons finely chopped parsley*
> *1/2 teaspoon dried cilantro*
> *Salt and pepper*
> *2 cups bottled salsa (hot, medium or mild)*
> *16-ounce can tomato sauce*

Bring a large pot of water to the boil for the pasta. Add salt and the lasagne noodles and boil for about 10 minutes or until al dente. Drain well.

(continued)

Cilantro is a green, leafy herb resembling flat Italian parsley. It has a slightly soapy, very distinctive flavor that is evident in a lot of Mexican cooking as well as in dishes created by chefs practicing what is referred to as "California cuisine." Cilantro is also known as coriander and Chinese parsley.

Meanwhile, in a mixing bowl, combine the ricotta with half the Monterey jack and half the cheddar cheese. Stir in the parsley and cilantro and add salt and pepper to taste.

In another mixing bowl, stir together the salsa and tomato sauce.

Lay the noodles on a flat surface and spread each one with 2 to 3 tablespoons of the cheese mixture. Roll up the noodles.

Spread a thin layer of the salsa mixture over the bottom of a buttered 9-by-13-inch baking dish. Lay the lasagne roll-ups seam side down and close together in the dish. Spoon the remaining salsa mixture over the roll-ups and sprinkle with the remaining Monterey jack and cheddar cheese. Cover the baking dish with foil.

Heat the oven to 350 degrees.

Bake the covered casserole for 30 to 40 minutes until heated through.

Let stand for 5 minutes, then use a spatula to remove the roll-ups, serving two to a portion and spooning sauce from the baking dish over each serving.

NOTE: The casserole may be made ahead of time or frozen. Heat the chilled or thawed casserole in a 350-degree oven for 45 to 50 minutes.

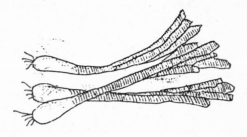

Crab-Stuffed Shells with Tarragon-Tomato Sauce

Serves 4 to 6

Fresh crabmeat is tastiest, but these elegant shells are good with frozen or canned crabmeat, too.

8 ounces jumbo pasta shells (about 40 shells)
8 ounces cream cheese, at room temperature
8 ounces (2 cups) fresh, frozen or canned
    crabmeat, picked over to remove cartilage
1/3 cup bread crumbs
1/4 cup finely chopped scallions, including green
    tops
1 teaspoon lemon juice
1/8 teaspoon ground nutmeg
1/8 teaspoon cayenne pepper

TARRAGON–TOMATO SAUCE:
2 16-ounce cans stewed tomatoes and their juice
1/2 cup white wine
2 teaspoons chopped fresh tarragon
    or 1/2 teaspoon dried
Freshly ground black pepper

Bring a large pot of water to the boil for the pasta. Add salt and cook the shells in rapidly boiling water for about 10 minutes until al dente. Drain in a colander, run cold water over the shells to stop their cooking and drain well on paper towels. There should be a few extra shells, so don't be concerned if a few of them break.

Combine the softened cream cheese and the crabmeat in a bowl with the bread crumbs, scallions, lemon juice, nutmeg and cayenne. Mix well and set aside.

To make the sauce, combine the stewed tomatoes and their juice with the wine and the tarragon. Bring to

The shells may be assembled early in the day or made ahead and frozen. Heat refrigerated or thawed shells covered with foil for about 45 minutes or until hot.

the boil, breaking up the stewed tomatoes with the side of a spoon. Reduce the heat and cook the sauce gently for 5 minutes.

Pour about half of the sauce in the bottom of a 9-by-13-inch pan.

Stuff the shells, using about 1 tablespoon of filling for each one. There should be enough of the crab mixture to fill about 30 shells. Arrange the shells, stuffed sides up, in the baking dish and pour the remaining sauce over the pasta. The sauce need not cover the shells completely. In fact, it is nice if some of their shape is still visible.

Heat the oven to 350 degrees.

Cover the baking dish with foil and bake for 25 to 30 minutes until heated through. Grind black pepper over the top before serving.

SUN-DRIED TOMATOES

A few years ago, sun-dried tomatoes were available only in specialty shops, packed in oil and very expensive. Now you can find them in many supermarket produce sections packaged dry, without oil.

Ravioli with Sun-Dried Tomato Sauce

Serves 6

Sun-dried tomatoes lend this dish a tang that conjures up the sunshine of the Italian Riviera. If the tomatoes you buy seem a little salty, rinse them in cold water before using.

> *1 pound frozen meat or cheese ravioli*
> *¼ cup olive oil*
> *1 onion, chopped*
> *2 ounces sun-dried tomatoes, chopped
>   (about ½ cup)*
> *28-ounce can crushed tomatoes in puree*
> *8-ounce can tomato sauce*
> *¼ cup red or white wine*
> *¼ teaspoon pepper*
> *2 tablespoons finely chopped fresh basil
>   or 2 teaspoons dried*
> *½ cup heavy cream*
> *Grated Parmesan cheese*

Bring a large pot of water to the boil for the pasta. Add salt and the ravioli and cook according to package directions. Drain well and return to the cooking pot to keep warm.

Meanwhile, make the sauce. Heat the oil in a large skillet or saucepan and cook the onion over medium-low heat for about 5 minutes until softened. Add the sun-dried tomatoes, crushed tomatoes, tomato sauce, wine and pepper. Cook gently, uncovered, for 10 minutes, stirring often. Stir in the basil and cream and cook 5 minutes more.

Serve the sauce spooned over the hot ravioli. Pass the Parmesan for sprinkling on top.

CHAPTER 6

PASTA AND VEGETABLES

Fresh, crisp vegetables, softly melting cheese and just-cooked pasta, quickly tossed and served right away, are a splendid meal. A glass of chilled white wine and a piece of bread might make the meal complete, but neither is necessary. Many vegetable and pasta dishes are perfect by themselves as a light, satisfying meal or as flavorful side dishes to highlight grilled fish, roast meat or chicken.

With the emphasis on healthy eating these days, many of us search for ways to prepare meatless meals or meals that require only a little meat. These pasta and vegetable dishes are the answer, whether the garden is lush with fresh squash, eggplant and peppers, or it is the dead of winter when we make do with frozen spinach and dried wild mushrooms.

With few exceptions, vegetable and pasta dishes are meant to be cooked shortly before eating, which makes them good candidates for weekday suppers when you want to make a nutritious and tasty meal quickly. They are also good choices for dinner parties and family get-togethers where they become colorful side dishes sure to catch the fancy of everyone who tries them.

Fettuccine with Spinach and Ricotta Sauce

Serves 6

The gentle flavor of ricotta melds deliciously with spinach and prosciutto to make a creamy sauce for fettuccine or other strand pasta. If you prefer a meatless meal, leave out the prosciutto.

1 pound fettuccine
1/4 cup olive oil
1 small onion, chopped
1 large clove garlic, finely chopped
10-ounce package chopped spinach, thawed and
*   squeezed of excess moisture*
3 ounces slivered prosciutto
1 cup (4 ounces) ricotta cheese
1 1/2 cups milk
1/2 teaspoon salt
1/2 teaspoon pepper
1/4 teaspoon grated nutmeg
1/4 cup (1 ounce) grated Parmesan cheese

Bring a large pot of water to the boil for the pasta. Add salt and the fettuccine and cook for about 9 minutes or until al dente. Drain well.

Meanwhile, heat the oil in a large skillet. Add the onion and cook gently for about 5 minutes over moderate-low heat until just softened. Add the garlic, spinach and prosciutto and cook, stirring, for 1 minute. Stir in the ricotta, milk, salt, pepper and nutmeg. Cook, stirring over very low heat, for 1 to 2 minutes until the mixture is heated through. Stir in the Parmesan. Taste and add salt and pepper if needed.

To serve, pour the sauce over the hot pasta and toss gently but thoroughly to coat.

Rosemary
Ratatouille Pasta

Serves 6

Rosemary, capers, garlic, eggplant, tomatoes. . .the
tastes of Provence, one of the most romantic and lovely
regions of France, come together in this classic vegetable medley. Tossing it with pretty corkscrew pasta
turns the ratatouille into a main dish.

The ratatouille can
be made a day
ahead of serving
(in fact, it may
taste even better
given the time to
blend) and there
is no need to peel
the eggplant.

> 5 tablespoons olive oil
> 1 large onion, halved and thinly sliced
> 3 cloves garlic, finely chopped
> 1 medium-size or 2 small zucchini (about 8
>   ounces), sliced
> 1 small eggplant (about 12 ounces), cut in
>   ¾-inch cubes
> 1 green bell pepper, seeded and cut in thin slices
> ½ teaspoon salt
> ½ teaspoon pepper
> 28-ounce can tomatoes in puree
> 2 teaspoons drained small capers
> 1 teaspoon dried rosemary
> 2 tablespoons finely chopped parsley
> 1 pound fusilli or other strand pasta
> Grated Parmesan cheese

Heat the oil in a large skillet or saucepan. Cook the
onion over medium-low heat for about 3 minutes. Add
the garlic, zucchini, eggplant, bell pepper, salt and pepper and cook about 5 minutes over medium-low heat.

Add the tomatoes, capers and rosemary. Cook, uncovered, over low heat for about 10 minutes, stirring to
break up the tomatoes, until the mixture is slightly
reduced and thickened. Stir in the parsley. Taste and
add salt and pepper as desired.

Bring a large pot of water to the boil for the pasta. Add salt and the fusilli and cook for about 12 minutes or until al dente. Drain well.

To serve, spoon the ratatouille over the pasta in a large deep platter or on individual plates. Pass the grated Parmesan.

GORGONZOLA

Although a good deal of the Gorgonzola we eat is American-made, it is authentically an Italian blue-veined cheese made from cow's milk and left to age until a natural mold appears. The Italian-made kind is always wrapped in gold foil and has a map of Italy on the label.

Rigatoni with Broccoli and Gorgonzola

Serves 6

Broccoli and garlic combine nicely in this easy, quick pasta dish. Substitute any large pasta for the rigatoni, such as ziti or mostaccioli.

1 pound rigatoni
6 cups broccoli florets (cut from 1 large bunch of broccoli)
6 tablespoons olive oil
4 large cloves garlic, finely chopped
1 cup (4 ounces) crumbled Gorgonzola cheese
Pepper

Rigatoni is a large tubular pasta with grooved sides— the sort of pasta best tossed with chunky sauces, not smooth, creamy ones.

(continued)

Bring a large pot of water to the boil for the pasta and broccoli. Add salt and the rigatoni and cook at a rapid boil for 8 minutes. Add the broccoli florets, bring back to the boil and cook for 3 minutes until the rigatoni is al dente and the broccoli is crisp-tender. Drain in a colander.

Heat the olive oil in a large skillet. Add the garlic and cook over low heat for 2 minutes. Combine the drained pasta and broccoli with the garlic oil, either in the skillet or in the pasta pot. Toss until the pasta and broccoli are well coated with oil and transfer to a warm serving bowl. Sprinkle with the Gorgonzola and the pepper, toss again and serve.

Pasta Primavera

Serves 6

Toss long, skinny strands of pasta with a bright, light sauce bursting with the fresh flavors of spring. Vermicelli or spaghettini are good choices for the pasta. The very thinnest pastas, such as capellini, easily overcook and may end up as a large, dense clump.

> *12 ounces slender asparagus*
> *1 medium (8 ounce) yellow crookneck squash*
> *1 pound vermicelli*
> *1 clove garlic, peeled and cut in half*
> *1½ cups thawed frozen peas*
> *1 red pepper, cut in small cubes*
> *1 cup thinly sliced scallions, including green tops*
> *1½ cups heavy cream*
> *1 cup (4 ounces) grated Parmesan cheese*

3 tablespoons chopped fresh basil
or 2 teaspoons dried
Freshly ground black pepper
Salt, if needed

Bring a large pot of water to the boil for the pasta and vegetables.

Break off and discard the tough bottoms of the asparagus stems. Slice the stems into ½-inch rounds, leaving the tips about 1 inch long. Cut the yellow squash into ½-inch dice.

Salt the water and add the vermicelli and the halved garlic. Cook at a rapid boil for 3 minutes. Add the sliced asparagus stems and tips and the yellow squash and cook for an additional 3 minutes until the pasta is al dente and the vegetables are crisp-tender. Drain in a colander and discard the garlic.

Return the drained pasta and vegetables to the pot and place over low heat. Add the peas, red pepper and scallions and toss until combined. Add the cream, Parmesan and basil and, using 2 large forks, toss the pasta until the cheese melts and a creamy sauce is formed. Grind on a generous amount of black pepper and add salt if desired. (Parmesan can be salty, so you may not want to add any.) Transfer to a warm serving bowl or serve on warm plates.

ROASTING PEPPERS

To bring out the sweetness of red or yellow bell peppers, try roasting them before tossing them with pasta. Put them under the broiler, turning then periodically as they char. When they are black on all sides, put the peppers in a paper bag to steam a little as they cool. Rub the charred skin off with your fingers. Resist the temptation to rinse the peppers in water—they quickly absorb the water and lose flavor.

Fettuccine with Goat Cheese and Swiss Chard

Serves 4 to 6

Swiss chard is a leafy vegetable that seems suddenly to overtake the garden. Wilting it in a little oil and tossing it with melting cheese converts it into a richly flavored sauce for strand pasta. Roasted walnuts add crunch and robust flavor that go very well with pasta and chard.

> 1 pound fettuccine
> 1/4 cup olive oil
> 12 cups lightly packed trimmed Swiss chard
>   leaves, washed, drained and cut into strips
> 3 1/2 cups heavy cream
> 2 1/2 cups (10 ounces) crumbled soft, mild goat
>   cheese or Gorgonzola cheese
> 1/2 cup coarsely chopped, toasted walnuts
> Pepper

Bring a large pot of water to the boil for the pasta. Add the fettuccine and cook at a rapid boil for 8 or 9 minutes or until al dente. Drain well.

Heat the oil in a large skillet over moderate heat. Add the chard and cook it for 2 to 3 minutes, just long enough for it to wilt. Add the cream, cheese and 1/4 cup of the walnuts. Cook over moderate heat until the cheese melts, tossing to mix the ingredients. Season the sauce with pepper.

Put the pasta in a warm bowl. Add the sauce and toss lightly. Sprinkle with the remaining nuts and serve at once.

CHAPTER 7

PASTA WITH SEAFOOD

One of the pleasures of serving pasta with seafood is that delicious, complete meals can be made in minutes—meals that are as fit for company as for the family. Hardly anyone objects to smoky salmon, juicy clams and sweet scallops tossed with their pasta. And why would they? Pasta and seafood, whether bound together with a rich cream sauce or a full-flavored tomato-based one, are the best of combinations.

Happily, seafood is more and more available to folks from landlocked regions of the country. Fresh clams, mussels and tender bay scallops are flown in daily to fish markets and the fish departments of supermarkets. Fresh fish and seafood is always preferable to frozen, so try to take advantage of it when you see it. Eat it the same day you buy it for a great tasting meal that will please your guests, your family and—because a relatively small amount of seafood goes a long way when mixed with pasta—your pocketbook.

Thin Linguine
with White Clam Sauce

Serves 6

White clam sauce is lighter and more delicate than red clam sauce and does nicely tossed with thin linguine or thin spaghetti. Many fish markets sell fresh chopped clams or you can use canned clams. The best-tasting sauce, of course, is made from fresh clams you shuck and chop yourself. Whichever you choose, be sure to save the clam juice to add to the sauce.

> 1 pound thin or regular linguine
> 3 cups drained chopped fresh clams or 3
>   10-ounce cans chopped clams, drained
> 2 cups clam juice (see note)
> 6 tablespoons olive oil
> 6 tablespoons (3 ounces) butter
> 4 cloves garlic, finely chopped
> 1/2 cup white wine
> 3/4 teaspoon dried thyme
> 1/4 teaspoon black pepper
> 1/2 cup finely chopped parsley
> Salt
>
> OPTIONAL GARNISH:
> 18 cherrystone clams, well scrubbed
> 1/2 cup white wine
> Grated Parmesan cheese

Bring a large pot of water to the boil for the pasta. Add salt and the linguine and cook for 6 to 8 minutes until al dente. Drain well.

Meanwhile, drain the chopped clams and measure and reserve the juices. Add enough bottled clam juice to the chopped clam liquid to make 2 cups.

Heat the oil and butter in a large skillet or saucepan. Add the garlic and cook gently for 1 minute. Add the clam juice, wine, thyme and pepper. Cook gently, uncovered, for 8 to 9 minutes until reduced by about one-quarter. Stir in the clams and all but 1 tablespoon of the parsley and cook for about 1 minute. Taste and add salt if desired. (Clam juice is quite salty, so none may be needed.)

If using the optional garnish, put the clams in a saucepan with the wine. Cover and steam for about 5 minutes until the clams open. Discard any that do not open. Remove the clams from the saucepan and pour ¼ cup of the cooking liquid into the sauce, taking care to leave any sediment in the saucepan.

Add the sauce to the hot pasta and toss gently but thoroughly. Turn the pasta into a large serving bowl or shallow individual bowls. Garnish with the whole steamed clams and sprinkle with the remaining tablespoon of parsley. Pass the Parmesan at the table.

NOTE: If you use chopped fresh clams, you should have about ½ cup juice. If you use canned clams, there will be more juice. Add bottled clam juice to the drained juice to make the required 2 cups.

Linguine with
Red Clam Sauce

Serves 6

Tossed with a judicious amount of clams, this hearty, zesty sauce is reminiscent of those served in trattorias in Manhattan's Little Italy. It deserves a bold, young Chianti and a good loaf of Italian bread. Spoon it over spaghetti or another strand pasta as well as linguine.

> 1/4 cup olive oil
> 2 cloves garlic, finely chopped
> 28-ounce can crushed tomatoes in puree
> 1 teaspoon dried marjoram or oregano
> 1/4 - 1/2 teaspoon dried red pepper flakes
> 3 cups drained chopped fresh clams or 3
>   10-ounce cans drained baby clams, juices
>   reserved
> 1/2 cup clam juice (see note)
> 1 teaspoon sugar
> Salt, if necessary
> 1 pound linguine
> Grated Parmesan cheese

Bring a large pot of water to the boil for the pasta.

Heat the olive oil in a large pot. Add the garlic and cook over low heat for 2 minutes. Add the tomatoes, raise the heat to moderate and cook, uncovered, for 10 minutes until the sauce is somewhat thickened. Add the marjoram, red pepper flakes, clams and clam juice and sugar. Continue to cook, uncovered, over moderate heat for 5 minutes. Taste for seasonings, adding additional red pepper flakes if the sauce is not hot enough. Add salt if desired, though the sauce should not need any because clams and their juice are usually quite salty.

Add salt to the pasta water and cook the linguine at a rapid boil for about 8 minutes or until al dente. Drain in a colander and transfer to a warm platter or divide among individual plates. Reheat the sauce if necessary and spoon it over the pasta. Pass the Parmesan at table.

NOTE: You should have about ½ cup of clam juice from the fresh chopped clams and a much greater quantity from the canned baby clams.

Fettuccine with Scallops, Citrus and Herbs

Serves 6

The fresh flavor of tarragon highlights the springtime goodness of asparagus in this elegant pasta dish.

1 cup white wine
1 clove garlic, peeled and crushed
1 pound bay scallops
1 cup cream
½ cup thinly sliced scallions, including green
  tops
1 tablespoon chopped fresh tarragon
  or 1 teaspoon dried
¾ teaspoon grated orange rind
½ teaspoon grated lemon rind
¾ teaspoon salt
¼ teaspoon pepper
1 pound fettuccine
12 ounces slender asparagus, stems trimmed and
  cut in ½-inch rounds, tips cut about 1½
  inches long
2 tablespoons (1 ounce) butter
Tarragon sprigs for garnish, if available

Bay scallops are smaller and usually a little more tender than sea scallops. If you cannot find them, use sea scallops, cut into quarters. They are good, too.

(continued)

Bring a large pot of water to the boil for the pasta and asparagus.

Put the wine and the crushed garlic in a medium-large saucepan and bring just to a simmer. Add the scallops and cook gently for 30 seconds until they are opaque. Remove the scallops to a bowl with a slotted spoon, leaving the garlic in the wine. Raise the heat to medium-high and cook, uncovered, for about 7 minutes, until the liquid is reduced to about ½ cup. Remove and discard the garlic clove.

Add the cream to the saucepan and cook, uncovered, over moderate heat for about 5 minutes until the sauce is somewhat thickened. Stir in the scallions, tarragon, orange and lemon rind, salt and pepper. Return the scallops and their liquid to the sauce and remove the saucepan from the heat.

Add salt to the pasta water and cook the fettuccine at a rapid boil for 6 minutes. Add the asparagus and cook for an additional 3 minutes until the pasta is al dente and the asparagus is almost tender. Drain in a colander and transfer the pasta and asparagus to a warm serving platter or divide among individual plates.

Reheat the scallops and sauce gently. Cut the butter into 4 pieces and stir it, one piece at a time, into the sauce. Spoon the sauce over the pasta and garnish with sprigs of tarragon if available.

PREPARING MUSSELS

Glossy black mussels often have a wiry "beard" extending from between their closed shell. The beard is easily removed by scrubbing the mussels with a wire brush or abrasive pad (without soap!) under cold running water.

Spaghetti with Mussels and Marinara Sauce

Serves 6

When Italian fishermen came in from a long day at sea they had little time to simmer a traditional red sauce, so they made a lusty, tomato-rich pasta sauce that could be eaten as it was or with pieces of seafood mixed in. Over the years, this style of sauce became known as Marinara sauce, named for the mariners who originated it. If you do not like the taste of anchovies, leave them out.

> 3 1/2 pounds fresh mussels (about 5 dozen)
> 1/2 cup white wine
> 3 tablespoons olive oil
> 2 large cloves garlic, finely chopped
> 2 28-ounce cans Italian plum tomatoes, drained
>   with juices reserved
> 2-ounce can anchovy fillets, undrained
> 1 tablespoon finely chopped fresh oregano
>   or 1 teaspoon dried
> 1/4 teaspoon pepper
> 1 pound spaghetti
> 3 tablespoons finely chopped parsley
> Salt
> Grated Parmesan cheese

Most anchovies are packed in oil, but some are sold packed in salt. These must be well rinsed before using.

Scrub and debeard the mussels. Put them in a large kettle and add the wine. Cover and steam for 3 to 5 minutes until the mussels open. Take the mussels from the pot and strain the cooking liquid through cheesecloth or a coffee filter and reserve. Set aside 12 mussels in the shell for garnish. Remove the remainder from the shells and reserve the mussel meat. Discard the shells.

Heat the olive oil in a large saucepan or kettle. Add the garlic and cook gently for 1 minute. Add the tomatoes, anchovies, oregano, pepper and reserved mussel cooking liquid. Cook gently, stirring often to break up the tomatoes and dissolve the anchovies, for 15 to 20 minutes until slightly thickened. If the sauce is too thick, add some of the reserved tomato liquid. (The sauce can be made a day ahead to this point.)

Meanwhile, bring a large pot of water to the boil for the pasta. Add salt and the spaghetti and cook for about 9 minutes until al dente. Drain well.

Just before serving, add the mussels and parsley to the simmering sauce. Cook for about 1 minute until the mussels are heated through. Taste and add salt if desired. Toss the sauce with the hot pasta and serve. Pass the Parmesan at the table.

CHAPTER 8

PASTA SALADS

Everyone loves pasta salads. In this chapter you will find salads made with shrimp and fresh herbs, a Greek pasta salad that includes feta cheese and tangy black olives, a filling tortellini salad and a salad that relies on spaghetti squash as well as spinach fettuccine. All are tasty, all are appropriate for a family supper or a buffet party.

Pasta salads are perfect make-ahead food. They benefit from a little standing time so that the flavors in their dressings have time to mingle and develop. Best served at room temperature, these versatile recipes can be assembled on a serving platter or bowl hours before the meal and taken from the refrigerator 30 minutes or so before dining. Both strand and shaped pastas do well in pasta salads—although they cannot be used interchangeably. Take heed of our suggestions as to the size and shape of the pasta and use your own good judgment as well.

Pasta salads are among the first dishes on a buffet table or picnic blanket to vanish. Make plenty—and experiment with your own mixtures of herbs and other ingredients. These colorful, bright dishes will become a permanent part of your repertoire.

Spaghetti Squash Pasta Salad with Basil Dressing

Serves 4 to 6

This recipe makes good use of the autumn harvest of squash and late tomatoes. The spaghetti squash tossed with the fettuccine provides interesting texture and taste and the sardines add zing.

Spaghetti squash is a winter squash with a pale yellow exterior and a stringy interior that, when cooked, looks very much like thin spaghetti. Cook the squash whole, covered with water, and simmer it for about 45 minutes. Cut it open, remove the seeds and carefully separate the flesh into the obvious strands.

> *4 ounces spinach fettuccine*
> *1 cup chopped tomatoes*
> *1/4 cup olive oil*
> *2 tablespoons lemon juice*
> *2 tablespoons chopped fresh basil*
> *or 2 teaspoons dried*
> *1 tablespoon snipped chives*
> *1 clove garlic, finely chopped*
> *Salt and pepper*
> *1 1/2 cups cooked spaghetti squash strands*
> *1 cup washed and torn spinach leaves*
> *2 3 3/4-ounce cans sardines in oil, drained*
> *Cherry tomatoes, for garnish*

Bring a large pot of water to the boil for the pasta. Cook the fettuccine at a rapid boil for 8 to 9 minutes until al dente. Drain well.

Combine the chopped tomatoes, olive oil, lemon juice, basil, chives, garlic and salt and pepper to taste in a large bowl.

Add the warm pasta to the dressing and toss to coat well. Add the squash and spinach leaves and toss gently. Transfer the salad to a serving platter. Lay the sardines on top of the salad and garnish with cherry tomatoes.

Tarragon-Thyme Shrimp and Orzo Salad

Serves 6

Tarragon and thyme blend deliciously to bring out the sweet flavor of fresh shrimp in this salad, which, because the vegetables are all about the same shape, is a good choice for a buffet.

TARRAGON-THYME DRESSING:
2 tablespoons white wine vinegar
2 teaspoons coarse-grain mustard
1 clove garlic, finely chopped
3 tablespoons vegetable oil
3 tablespoons olive oil
3 tablespoons chopped fresh tarragon or 1 tablespoon dried
1 tablespoon chopped fresh thyme or 1 teaspoon dried
3/4 teaspoon salt
1/2 teaspoon black pepper

SALAD:
8 ounces (1 cup) orzo or other small pasta
12 ounces medium shrimp, peeled and deveined
8 ounces plum tomatoes, cored, seeded and chopped into small pieces
1 cup frozen corn kernels, thawed
3/4 cup thinly sliced scallions, including green tops
1/2 cup diced red pepper
1/2 cup thinly sliced celery
Sprigs of the fresh herbs, if available, for garnish

Buy shrimp in the shells to insure they will be as fresh as can be. Figure that the shells about double the weight of the shrimp—if you need 12 ounces of shelled shrimp, buy 24 ounces of shrimp in the shell.

Bring a large pot of water to the boil for the pasta. To make the dressing, whisk together the vinegar and mustard in a small bowl. Add the garlic and gradually whisk in the oils. Stir in the herbs and the salt and pepper.

Add salt to the water and cook the orzo in rapidly boiling water for 6 minutes. Add the shrimp and cook for an additional 2 minutes. Drain in a colander and run cold water over the orzo and shrimp to stop their cooking. Drain well and transfer to a large bowl. Add the tomatoes, corn, scallions, red pepper and celery and toss to combine.

Pour the dressing over the salad and toss gently to coat well. Serve immediately or chill for up to 8 hours. Garnish with the herb sprigs before serving.

Greek Chicken and Pasta Salad

Serves 6

The black olives and the salty feta cheese give this salad its name. Try it with shrimp rather than chicken, or leave out the meat altogether and serve it as an accompaniment to grilled meats and poultry.

DRESSING:
2 tablespoons lemon juice
2 tablespoons red wine vinegar
1 clove garlic, finely chopped
2 tablespoons finely chopped fresh dill
    or 2 teaspoons dried
1/2 teaspoon black pepper
1/2 teaspoon salt
3/4 cup olive oil

SALAD:

10 ounces cavatelli, short twists or farfalle
3 cups bite-sized pieces of cooked chicken or
  turkey (about 1 pound)
1 cup (4 ounces) crumbled feta cheese
1/2 seedless cucumber, thinly sliced
1 yellow bell pepper, cut into 1/4-inch pieces
1/4 cup sliced scallions, including green tops

GARNISH:
6 cherry tomatoes, halved
1/2 cup Greek olives
Dill sprigs

Bring a large pot of water to the boil for the pasta.

To make the dressing, whisk together the lemon juice, vinegar, garlic, dill, pepper and salt. Whisk in the oil until well blended. Reserve for up to 4 hours until needed. Whisk again to reblend before using.

To make the salad, add salt and the cavatelli to the boiling water and cook for about 12 minutes or until al dente. Drain well in a colander, then run under cold water to stop the cooking.

In a large mixing bowl, combine the pasta, chicken, cheese, cucumber, bell pepper and scallions. Add the dressing and toss gently to combine. The salad may be served immediately or chilled for up to 6 hours. Remove from the refrigerator 30 minutes before garnishing and serving.

To serve, spoon the salad into a decorative shallow dish or onto individual plates. Garnish with the tomatoes, olives and dill sprigs.

Most feta cheese is made from goats' milk, although some is made from cows' and sheep's milk, too. It is tangy fresh cheese, packed in brine and very salty. Rinse it when you get it home and keep it covered with cold water in the refrigerator to cut down on the saltiness.

Tortellini Salad with Three-Herb Dressing

Serves 6

A bold-tasting pasta salad made with cheese tortellini, this is a terrific party dish. The basil, parsley and chives lend it garden-fresh flavor and pretty green color.

You can also make this dressing in a bowl, beating thoroughly with a wire whisk, provided all the fresh herbs have been chopped finely beforehand.

THREE-HERB DRESSING:
2 tablespoons red wine vinegar
1 tablespoon lemon juice
2 teaspoons Dijon mustard
1 cup packed parsley sprigs
*1/3 cup packed, torn fresh basil leaves
   or 5 teaspoons dried*
1/2 cup olive oil
*1/4 cup chopped chives or finely chopped scallion
   tops*
3/4 teaspoon salt
1/2 teaspoon pepper

SALAD:
1 pound frozen cheese tortellini
4 ounces prosciutto, cut in thin strips
*2 firm ripe tomatoes, cored and each cut
   in 6 wedges*
Salt
Black pepper

Bring a large pot of water to the boil for the pasta.
   To make the dressing, put the vinegar, lemon juice and mustard in the workbowl of a food processor. Pulse once to combine. Add the parsley and basil and turn the machine on. With the motor running, pour the oil slowly through the feed tube until a thick dressing is formed. Stop the motor once to scrape down the sides.

Add the chives, salt and pepper and pulse once or twice to combine.

Add salt to the pasta water and cook the tortellini at a rapid boil for about 5 minutes or according to package directions until al dente. Drain in a colander, rinse under cold running water to stop the cooking and drain again.

Put the pasta and prosciutto in a bowl, pour the dressing over the tortellini and toss to coat. Serve immediately or chill for up to 8 hours before serving. Remove from the refrigerator about 30 minutes before serving.

Transfer to a rimmed platter, garnish with the tomato wedges and sprinkle the tomatoes with salt and pepper.

Curried Chicken and Pasta Salad

Serves 6

Have you tried curry lately? This mild curried chicken salad is a good choice as a side dish for a party, or as a main course anytime. It is also good made with leftover grilled or roasted lamb.

CURRY DRESSING:
1 cup mayonnaise
3/4 cup plain yogurt
3 tablespoons chopped chutney
1 1/2 teaspoons curry powder
3/4 teaspoon black pepper
1/2 teaspoon salt

(continued)

SALAD:

12 ounces rotelle, short pasta twists or shells
3 cups broccoli florets
3 cups bite-sized pieces of cooked chicken or
turkey (about 1 pound)
1 red bell pepper, cut in ¼-inch pieces
1 small Golden or Red Delicious apple, cored
and cut in ¼-inch slices

To make the dressing, combine all the ingredients in a mixing bowl. Chill for at least 15 minutes to blend the flavors.

To make the salad, bring a large pot of water to the boil for the pasta. Add salt and the rotelle and boil 7 minutes. Add the broccoli and boil about 2 minutes until the florets are crisp-tender and the pasta is al dente. Drain well in a colander, then run cold water over the pasta and broccoli to stop their cooking.

Turn the pasta and broccoli into a large mixing bowl. Add the chicken and bell pepper. Pour the dressing over the mixture and toss gently until coated.

The salad may be served immediately or chilled for up to 6 hours. Remove from the refrigerator 30 minutes before garnishing with the apple slices and serving.

Cold Sesame-Ginger Noodles

Serves 6

Serve this at your next party or family gathering and you will be deluged with requests for the recipe. It is a refreshing change from the usual as it introduces some of the pungent tastes of Asia to the table. If you can get quick-cooking Oriental noodles, use them; if not, whole wheat pasta or vermicelli does very well. For this recipe you will need a pound of Oriental noodles—cook them according to the package directions.

SESAME-GINGER DRESSING:

2 tablespoons red wine vinegar

2 tablespoons soy sauce

2 tablespoons peanut butter

3 teaspoons finely chopped fresh ginger

2 cloves garlic, finely chopped

2 teaspoons sugar

¼ cup vegetable oil

2 tablespoons sesame oil

½ teaspoon red pepper flakes

SALAD:

12 ounces whole wheat or regular vermicelli or other thin-strand noodle, broken into 4-inch lengths

4 ounces snow peas (30-40), strings removed, cut in half diagonally if very large

6 ounces baked or smoked ham, cut in thin strips

1 cup thinly sliced scallions, including green tops

Coarsely ground black pepper

(continued)

Bring a large pot of water to the boil for the pasta.

To make the dressing, whisk together the vinegar, soy sauce, peanut butter, ginger, garlic and sugar in a small bowl. Gradually whisk in the vegetable oil and the sesame oil and season with the red pepper flakes.

Add salt to the pasta water and cook the noodles in rapidly boiling water for about 6 minutes until al dente. Add the snow peas for the last 30 seconds of the cooking time. Drain the noodles and the snow peas in a colander, run cold water over them to stop the cooking and drain well. Transfer to a bowl. Add the slivered ham and the scallions and toss.

Pour the dressing over the noodles and toss gently but thoroughly until they are well coated with dressing. Cover and chill for at least 1 hour or for as long as 24 hours. Toss again before serving.

Transfer to a deep-rimmed platter, making sure that some of the snow peas are on the top. Sprinkle liberally with black pepper and serve.